Contents

Some words are shown in bold, **like this**.
You can find them in the glossary on page 23.

When will I start at a new school?

All children have a first day at school.

Most children start school for the first time when they have finished nursery or pre-school.

Older children also sometimes start at a new school.

If you move house or go to a middle school then you will go to a new school.

What do I need to take to school?

When you go to school you'll need to take a coat if the weather is cold or wet.

You'll also need a bag to carry books and letters to and from school.

You might need to take a packed lunch unless you are having school dinners.

You do not need to take toys to school as everything you need will be in your classroom.

How do I get to school?

If you live near your school you may walk to school with an adult.

Walking to school is a good way to get **exercise** in the morning.

If you live further away you might get a school bus.

Some children travel to school by car.

What happens when I get to school?

When you get to school you will see lots of other children in the playground.

The teachers will open the door when it is time to go in.

Everyone goes into school and finds their own peg.

When you have put away your things you can go into your new classroom.

What happens in my classroom?

All schools start the day in different ways.

In many schools your teacher will meet you as you come into the classroom.

You might start the day by sitting down together and greeting each other.

Your teacher will probably take the **register**.

What do I need to know?

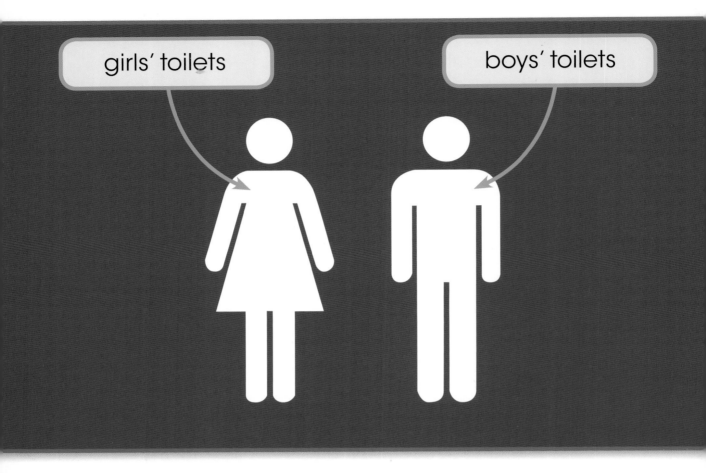

It's important to know your way around your new school.

You need to know where the toilets and your peg are.

You also need to know the names of the teachers and where your classroom is.

Don't be afraid to ask for help if you are not sure about anything.

What will happen during the day?

The school day will be different in all schools.

You will get to know the other children as you work and play together.

Many schools have a snack time, lunch time, and play time during the day.

There might be an **assembly** with the rest of the school or some other classes.

Is it OK to be nervous?

Most children feel nervous when they start a new school for the first time.

There will be other children who feel the same as you.

Tell your teacher if you feel unhappy.

He or she will help you make friends and find something to do that you enjoy.

What happens at the end of the day?

At the end of the day your class might come together to say goodbye.

Then you will need to collect all of your things before leaving the classroom.

Sometimes children go home on a school bus.

Others are collected by their parents or another carer.

School tips

Do:

- ✓ listen carefully and quietly to your teacher

- ✓ put your hand up to speak

- ✓ be kind to other children

- ✓ have fun!

Don't:

- ✗ run in the school building

- ✗ be afraid to ask if you are not sure about anything

- ✗ forget to try your best.

Picture glossary

 **assembly** meeting for everyone in school

 **exercise** sport or activity. Running and walking are good ways of getting some exercise.

 **register** list of names the teacher checks at the start of the day

Find out more

Books

I Am Too Absolutely Small for School, Lauren Child (Orchard, 2007)

Lucy and Tom Go to School, Martha Shirley Hughes (Puffin, 1996)

Where's My Peg?: My First Day at School, Jen Green (Wayland, 2007)

Websites

Follow the link for "Starting school" which will tell you what to expect on your first day at a new school:
http://www.cyh.com/Archive/NewsDetail. aspx?p=260&id=2354&np=274

Index